W0017755

# The Travel Nurse Assignment Organizer

by

Karie Peters

# Hello My Fellow Travelers!

Congratulations on choosing my favorite career path to date. Here we are! What better way to combine our love of traveling with a career? Whether you're a Travel Nurse, CNA, Respiratory Therapist or NP (you get the idea), this book is for you!

You should know, traveling is NOT for everybody; however, if it is for you, you will absolutely love it! And, you will also soon discover that there is a lot of information with which to keep up. During my journey I have switched between multiple agencies for various reasons. You must be flexible and willing to seek out the perfect location that God has planned for you. But, trying to figure out where to stash all this information inside of my phone drove me crazy. I never lost my phone, but I can't tell you how many notes in my phone would get lost or repeated again and again in different places.

My Travel Buddy, you now hold the key to this mess in your hands! On the following pages, you will have the opportunity to document the necessary information, have it easily accessible, and take it with you everywhere you go. You'll find this same information is needed repeatedly on all of the applications you will be filling out for all your future assignments.

Remember why you do what you do. Enjoy your experiences and those you will meet along the way. This is a wonderful adventure, but keep in mind: this career is beautifully constructed to help other people across the country – and, later, if you're lucky enough – the world!

Good Luck and Safe Travels!

Karie

Only those
who risk
going too far
can possibly find out
how far
one can go.
- Thomas Stearns Eliot

# Thanks!

Without God, none of this would be possible. Straight up. He has taken care of us every step of our travel journey and beyond. A special appreciation to those fellow creators mentioned in this book. However, I could not have compiled them all without the help of a special few: Glen & Margaret Witt, Derek & Christee Witt, Kyle and Sarah. Nocona, thanks for the gorgeous front cover picture you took, and for putting up with us constantly being somewhere different all of the time.

Todd, nothing would have been possible without your help and attention to finite detail time and time again through the million editing sessions. Also, thank you Todd for seeing my vision and taking the back cover photo.

Special shoutout to Calvin and the crew at 104 Customs and More – I would still be fighting my cover design if it wasn't for you! Thanks for the amazing cover!

As always, a special thanks to the reader. Without your help and deciding to give this book a chance, this information could not get out! I hope this helps you keep your life together as much as it was able to help me!

Thanks to each of you for the awesome support!

*I'm in love with cities I've never been to and people I've never met.*

*– Melody Truong*

I'm going
on an
adventure!

– Bilbo Baggins

# Table of Contents

Assignments...................................................... 14-93

Top Five Assignments...................................... 95

Current References......................................... 96-97

About the Author............................................ 99

*Give every day the chance to become the most beautiful day of your life. – Mark Twain*

Then I heard the voice
of the Lord saying,
"Whom shall I send?
And who will go for us?"
And I said,
"Here am I. Send me."

– Isaiah 6:8

# Assignment No. \_\_\_\_

Facility Name: _____

Location: _____

Department: _____

Dates: _____

| Magnet Hospital?   Y/N |
| --- |
| Teaching Facility?   Y/N |
| Traveler Friendly?  Y/N |
| Receive an Extension Offer? (YAY!!!!)     Y/N |
| Did you Accept the Extension Offer?   Y/N |
| Would you return? Y/N |

Travel Agency: _____     Recruiter: _____

Recruiter Contact Info: _____   _____

                       (phone)                             (e-mail)

Contract Duration _____ weeks

Additional Contract weeks extended _____

Charting System Used: _____  Charge Nurse Experience? Y / N

Floated to These Units: _____

Facility Address:

*I was here....*

My temporary home address was....

**BEST** parts about this assignment:

- ➢
- ➢
- ➢

*Failure is not fatal, but failure to change might be.*

*— John Wooden*

# Assignment No. ____

Facility Name: _____

Location: _____

Department: _____

Dates: _____

Magnet Hospital?   Y/N

Teaching Facility?   Y/N

Traveler Friendly?   Y/N

Receive an Extension Offer? (YAY!!!!)     Y/N

Did you Accept the Extension Offer?   Y/N

Would you return? Y/N

Travel Agency: _____   Recruiter: _____

Recruiter Contact Info: _____   _____
                                (phone)                              (e-mail)

Contract Duration _____ weeks

Additional Contract weeks extended _____

Charting System Used: _____   Charge Nurse Experience? Y / N

Floated to These Units: _____

Facility Address:

*I was here....*

My temporary home address was....

**BEST** parts about this assignment:

➤

➤

➤

*Alone, we can do so little; together we can do so much.*

*– Helen Keller*

# Assignment No. _____

Magnet Hospital?   Y/N

Teaching Facility?   Y/N

Traveler Friendly?  Y/N

Receive an Extension
Offer? (YAY!!!!)     Y/N

Did you Accept the
Extension Offer?    Y/N

Would you return? Y/N

Facility Name: _____

Location: _____

Department: _____

Dates: _____

Travel Agency: _____   Recruiter: _____

Recruiter Contact Info: _____   _____

(phone)                                    (e-mail)

Contract Duration _____ weeks

Additional Contract weeks extended _____

Charting System Used: _____   Charge Nurse Experience? Y / N

Floated to These Units: _____

Facility Address:

I was here.....

My temporary home address was....

**BEST** parts about this assignment:

➢

➢

➢

*You can't stay in your corner of the Forest waiting for others to come to you. You have to go to them sometimes. — Winnie the Pooh*

# Assignment No. _____

Facility Name: _____

Location: _____

Department: _____

Dates: _____

Magnet Hospital?   Y/N

Teaching Facility?   Y/N

Traveler Friendly?   Y/N

Receive an Extension Offer? (YAY!!!!)     Y/N

Did you Accept the Extension Offer?   Y/N

Would you return? Y/N

Travel Agency: _____   Recruiter: _____

Recruiter Contact Info: _____   _____
                                (phone)                                    (e-mail)

Contract Duration _____ weeks

Additional Contract weeks extended _____

Charting System Used: _____   Charge Nurse Experience? Y / N

Floated to These Units: _____

Facility Address:

thank you

I was here....

My temporary home address was....

BEST parts about this assignment:

➢

➢

➢

*Travel is fatal to prejudice, bigotry, and narrow-mindedness. — Mark Twain*

# Assignment No. ____

Facility Name: _____

Location: _____

Department: _____

Dates: _____

Travel Agency: _____  Recruiter: _____

Recruiter Contact Info: _____  _____
                              (phone)                              (e-mail)

Contract Duration _____ weeks

Additional Contract weeks extended _____

Charting System Used: _____  Charge Nurse Experience? Y / N

Floated to These Units: _____

Facility Address:

| Magnet Hospital? Y/N |
| Teaching Facility? Y/N |
| Traveler Friendly? Y/N |
| Receive an Extension Offer? (YAY!!!!) Y/N |
| Did you Accept the Extension Offer? Y/N |
| Would you return? Y/N |

*I was here....*

My temporary home address was....

**BEST** parts about this assignment:

➤

➤

➤

*All journeys have secret destinations of which the traveler is unaware. – Martin Buber*

# Assignment No. _____

Facility Name: _____

Location: _____

Department: _____

Dates: _____

<table>
<tr><td>Magnet Hospital?   Y/N</td></tr>
<tr><td>Teaching Facility?   Y/N</td></tr>
<tr><td>Traveler Friendly?   Y/N</td></tr>
<tr><td>Receive an Extension Offer? (YAY!!!!)     Y/N</td></tr>
<tr><td>Did you Accept the Extension Offer?   Y/N</td></tr>
<tr><td>Would you return? Y/N</td></tr>
</table>

Travel Agency: _____     Recruiter: _____

Recruiter Contact Info: _____   _____

                  (phone)                                 (e-mail)

Contract Duration _____ weeks

Additional Contract weeks extended _____

Charting System Used: _____ Charge Nurse Experience? Y / N

Floated to These Units: _____

Facility Address:

you
make a
A DIFFERENCE

*I was here....*

My temporary home address was....

**BEST** parts about this assignment:

➢

➢

➢

*Let all that you do be done in love.*

*– 1 Cor 16:14*

# Assignment No. _____

| Magnet Hospital?   Y/N |
| Teaching Facility?   Y/N |
| Traveler Friendly?   Y/N |
| Receive an Extension Offer? (YAY!!!!)     Y/N |
| Did you Accept the Extension Offer?   Y/N |
| Would you return? Y/N |

Facility Name: _____

Location: _____

Department: _____

Dates: _____

Travel Agency: _____ Recruiter: _____

Recruiter Contact Info: _____ _____
                              (phone)                              (e-mail)

Contract Duration _____ weeks

Additional Contract weeks extended _____

Charting System Used: _____ Charge Nurse Experience? Y / N

Floated to These Units: _____

Facility Address:

you are awesome

*I was here.....*

My temporary home address was....

**BEST** parts about this assignment:

  ➢

  ➢

  ➢

*Nobody else can live the life you live.*

*– Mr. Rogers*

# Assignment No. ____

Facility Name: _____

Location: _____

Department: _____

Dates: _____

| Magnet Hospital?   Y/N |
|---|
| Teaching Facility?   Y/N |
| Traveler Friendly?   Y/N |
| Receive an Extension Offer? (YAY!!!!)     Y/N |
| Did you Accept the Extension Offer?   Y/N |
| Would you return? Y/N |

Travel Agency: _____     Recruiter: _____

Recruiter Contact Info: _____     _____
                            (phone)                          (e-mail)

Contract Duration _____ weeks

Additional Contract weeks extended _____

Charting System Used: _____     Charge Nurse Experience? Y / N

Floated to These Units: _____

Facility Address:

*you ARE Strong*

*I was here....*

My temporary home address was....

BEST parts about this assignment:

➢

➢

➢

*Sometimes I inspire my patients; more often they inspire me. – Unknown*

# Assignment No. _____

Facility Name: _____

Location: _____

Department: _____

Dates: _____

Magnet Hospital?   Y/N

Teaching Facility?   Y/N

Traveler Friendly?  Y/N

Receive an Extension
Offer? (YAY!!!!)    Y/N

Did you Accept the
Extension Offer?   Y/N

Would you return? Y/N

Travel Agency: _____    Recruiter: _____

Recruiter Contact Info: _____    _____
                                    (phone)                                    (e-mail)

Contract Duration _____ weeks

Additional Contract weeks extended _____

Charting System Used: _____    Charge Nurse Experience? Y / N

Floated to These Units: _____

Facility Address:

take a
small
step
EVERYDAY

# I was here....

My temporary home address was....

**BEST** parts about this assignment:

➤

➤

➤

*Adventure is out there!*

*– Charles Muntz, Up*

# Assignment No. _____

Facility Name: _____

Location: _____

Department: _____

Dates: _____

Magnet Hospital?   Y/N

Teaching Facility?   Y/N

Traveler Friendly?   Y/N

Receive an Extension
Offer? (YAY!!!!)     Y/N

Did you Accept the
Extension Offer?   Y/N

Would you return? Y/N

Travel Agency: _____  Recruiter: _____

Recruiter Contact Info: _____  _____
                                    (phone)                                                    (e-mail)

Contract Duration _____ weeks

Additional Contract weeks extended _____

Charting System Used: _____  Charge Nurse Experience? Y / N

Floated to These Units: _____

Facility Address:

*I was here....*

My temporary home address was....

BEST parts about this assignment:

➢

➢

➢

*God, in his sovereignty, never does anything that is not perfect, so be thankful no matter what comes your way!  – Glen Witt*

# Assignment No. _____

Facility Name: _____

Location: _____

Department: _____

Dates: _____

| |
|---|
| Magnet Hospital?   Y/N |
| Teaching Facility?   Y/N |
| Traveler Friendly?  Y/N |
| Receive an Extension Offer? (YAY!!!!)     Y/N |
| Did you Accept the Extension Offer?   Y/N |
| Would you return? Y/N |

Travel Agency: _____   Recruiter: _____

Recruiter Contact Info: _____   _____
                              (phone)                          (e-mail)

Contract Duration _____ weeks

Additional Contract weeks extended _____

Charting System Used: _____  Charge Nurse Experience? Y / N

Floated to These Units: _____

Facility Address:

*I was here....*

My temporary home address was....

**BEST** parts about this assignment:

➢

➢

➢

*With age comes wisdom. With travel, comes understanding.*

*-Sandra Lake*

# Assignment No. _____

Facility Name: _____

Location: _____

Department: _____

Dates: _____

| Magnet Hospital?  Y/N |
| --- |
| Teaching Facility?  Y/N |
| Traveler Friendly?  Y/N |
| Receive an Extension Offer? (YAY!!!!)    Y/N |
| Did you Accept the Extension Offer?   Y/N |
| Would you return? Y/N |

Travel Agency: _____    Recruiter: _____

Recruiter Contact Info: _____   _____
                              (phone)                                    (e-mail)

Contract Duration _____ weeks

Additional Contract weeks extended _____

Charting System Used: _____   Charge Nurse Experience? Y / N

Floated to These Units: _____

Facility Address:

I was here....

My temporary home address was....

BEST parts about this assignment:

➢

➢

➢

*Not all those who wander are lost.*

*- J.R.R. Tolkien*

# Assignment No. ____

Facility Name: _____

Location: _____

Department: _____

Dates: _____

Magnet Hospital?   Y/N

Teaching Facility?   Y/N

Traveler Friendly?  Y/N

Receive an Extension Offer? (YAY!!!!)     Y/N

Did you Accept the Extension Offer?   Y/N

Would you return? Y/N

Travel Agency: _____ Recruiter: _____

Recruiter Contact Info: _____ _____
                              (phone)                              (e-mail)

Contract Duration _____ weeks

Additional Contract weeks extended _____

Charting System Used: _____ Charge Nurse Experience? Y / N

Floated to These Units: _____

Facility Address:

*I was here.....*

My temporary home address was....

**BEST** parts about this assignment:

➢

➢

➢

*Kindness seeks to give – without thought or condition of return. – Candace Cameron Bure*

# Assignment No. _____

Magnet Hospital?   Y/N

Teaching Facility?   Y/N

Traveler Friendly?  Y/N

Receive an Extension
Offer? (YAY!!!!)     Y/N

Did you Accept the
Extension Offer?   Y/N

Would you return? Y/N

Facility Name:   _____

Location:   _____

Department: _____

Dates: _____

Travel Agency: _____  Recruiter: _____

Recruiter Contact Info: _____  _____

(phone)                                     (e-mail)

Contract Duration _____ weeks

Additional Contract weeks extended _____

Charting System Used: _____  Charge Nurse Experience? Y / N

Floated to These Units: _____

Facility Address:

I was here....

My temporary home address was....

BEST parts about this assignment:

> 

> 

> 

All your life, you will be faced with a choice. You can choose love or hate. I choose love. – Johnny Cash

# Assignment No. _____

| |
|---|
| Magnet Hospital?   Y/N |
| Teaching Facility?   Y/N |
| Traveler Friendly?   Y/N |
| Receive an Extension Offer? (YAY!!!!)     Y/N |
| Did you Accept the Extension Offer?   Y/N |
| Would you return? Y/N |

Facility Name: _____

Location: _____

Department: _____

Dates: _____

Travel Agency: _____    Recruiter: _____

Recruiter Contact Info: _____    _____

                                 (phone)                                               (e-mail)

Contract Duration _____ weeks

Additional Contract weeks extended _____

Charting System Used: _____    Charge Nurse Experience? Y / N

Floated to These Units: _____

Facility Address:

You are making a difference Everyday

I was here....

My temporary home address was....

**BEST** parts about this assignment:

➢

➢

➢

*You must go on adventures to find out where you truly belong. – Sue Fitzmaurice*

# Assignment No. _____

Facility Name: _____

Location: _____

Department: _____

Dates: _____

Magnet Hospital?   Y/N

Teaching Facility?   Y/N

Traveler Friendly?  Y/N

Receive an Extension
Offer? (YAY!!!!)     Y/N

Did you Accept the
Extension Offer?   Y/N

Would you return? Y/N

Travel Agency: _____    Recruiter: _____

Recruiter Contact Info: _____    _____
                              (phone)                        (e-mail)

Contract Duration _____ weeks

Additional Contract weeks extended _____

Charting System Used: _____    Charge Nurse Experience? Y / N

Floated to These Units: _____

Facility Address:

just keep going

*I was here....*

My temporary home address was....

**BEST** parts about this assignment:

> ➢

> ➢

> ➢

*It isn't what we say or think that defines us, but what we do.*

*— Jane Austen, Sense & Sensibility*

# Assignment No. _____

Magnet Hospital?   Y/N

Teaching Facility?   Y/N

Traveler Friendly?   Y/N

Receive an Extension Offer? (YAY!!!!)     Y/N

Did you Accept the Extension Offer?   Y/N

Would you return? Y/N

Facility Name: _____

Location: _____

Department: _____

Dates: _____

Travel Agency: _____     Recruiter: _____

Recruiter Contact Info: _____     _____
                                    (phone)                                        (e-mail)

Contract Duration _____ weeks

Additional Contract weeks extended _____

Charting System Used: _____     Charge Nurse Experience? Y / N

Floated to These Units: _____

Facility Address:

Trust YOUR Talent

I was here....

My temporary home address was....

**BEST** parts about this assignment:

➢

➢

➢

*To know even one life has breathed easier because you have lived: that is to have succeeded. – Ralph Emerson*

# Assignment No. _____

Facility Name: _____

Location: _____

Department: _____

Dates: _____

| Magnet Hospital? Y/N |
| --- |
| Teaching Facility? Y/N |
| Traveler Friendly? Y/N |
| Receive an Extension Offer? (YAY!!!!) Y/N |
| Did you Accept the Extension Offer? Y/N |
| Would you return? Y/N |

Travel Agency: _____   Recruiter: _____

Recruiter Contact Info: _____   _____
                              (phone)                                    (e-mail)

Contract Duration _____ weeks

Additional Contract weeks extended _____

Charting System Used: _____   Charge Nurse Experience? Y / N

Floated to These Units: _____

Facility Address:

I was here....

My temporary home address was....

**BEST** parts about this assignment:

> 

> 

> 

We can make our plans, but the Lord determines our steps.

- Prov 16:9

# Assignment No. _____

Magnet Hospital?   Y/N

Teaching Facility?   Y/N

Traveler Friendly?   Y/N

Receive an Extension
Offer? (YAY!!!!)     Y/N

Did you Accept the
Extension Offer?   Y/N

Would you return? Y/N

Facility Name:   _____

Location:   _____

Department:   _____

Dates:   _____

Travel Agency: _____   Recruiter: _____

Recruiter Contact Info: _____   _____

(phone)                              (e-mail)

Contract Duration _____ weeks

Additional Contract weeks extended _____

Charting System Used: _____   Charge Nurse Experience? Y / N

Floated to These Units: _____

Facility Address:

*I was here....*

My temporary home address was....

**BEST** parts about this assignment:

➤

➤

➤

*If I cannot do great things, I can do small things in a great way. – Rev. Dr. Martin Luther King, Jr.*

# Assignment No. ____

Facility Name: _____

Location: _____

Department: _____

Dates: _____

<table>
<tr><td>Magnet Hospital?   Y/N</td></tr>
<tr><td>Teaching Facility?   Y/N</td></tr>
<tr><td>Traveler Friendly?   Y/N</td></tr>
<tr><td>Receive an Extension Offer? (YAY!!!!)     Y/N</td></tr>
<tr><td>Did you Accept the Extension Offer?   Y/N</td></tr>
<tr><td>Would you return? Y/N</td></tr>
</table>

Travel Agency: _____     Recruiter: _____

Recruiter Contact Info: _____     _____
                              (phone)                          (e-mail)

Contract Duration _____ weeks

Additional Contract weeks extended _____

Charting System Used: _____ Charge Nurse Experience? Y / N

Floated to These Units: _____

Facility Address:

Be the change you want to see

I was here....

My temporary home address was....

BEST parts about this assignment:

➢

➢

➢

*Strive not to be a success, but rather to be of value.*

*- Albert Einstein*

# Assignment No. _____

Magnet Hospital?   Y/N

Teaching Facility?   Y/N

Traveler Friendly?   Y/N

Receive an Extension
Offer? (YAY!!!!)     Y/N

Did you Accept the
Extension Offer?   Y/N

Would you return? Y/N

Facility Name: _____

Location: _____

Department: _____

Dates: _____

Travel Agency: _____   Recruiter: _____

Recruiter Contact Info: _____   _____
                                    (phone)                                              (e-mail)

Contract Duration _____ weeks

Additional Contract weeks extended _____

Charting System Used: _____   Charge Nurse Experience? Y / N

Floated to These Units: _____

Facility Address:

*I was here....*

My temporary home address was....

**BEST** parts about this assignment:

➢

➢

➢

*I attribute my success to this: I never gave nor took any excuse.*

*— Florence Nightingale*

# Assignment No. _____

Facility Name: _____

Location: _____

Department: _____

Dates: _____

<table>
<tr><td>Magnet Hospital?   Y/N</td></tr>
<tr><td>Teaching Facility?   Y/N</td></tr>
<tr><td>Traveler Friendly?  Y/N</td></tr>
<tr><td>Receive an Extension Offer? (YAY!!!!)     Y/N</td></tr>
<tr><td>Did you Accept the Extension Offer?    Y/N</td></tr>
<tr><td>Would you return? Y/N</td></tr>
</table>

Travel Agency: _____   Recruiter: _____

Recruiter Contact Info: _____   _____
                                    (phone)                                (e-mail)

Contract Duration _____ weeks

Additional Contract weeks extended _____

Charting System Used: _____   Charge Nurse Experience? Y / N

Floated to These Units: _____

Facility Address:

time
to
Relax

I was here....

My temporary home address was....

**BEST** parts about this assignment:

➢

➢

➢

*Have a heart that never hardens, a temper that never tires, a touch that never hurts. – Charles Dickens*

# Assignment No. _____

Facility Name: _____

Location: _____

Department: _____

Dates: _____

| Magnet Hospital?   Y/N |
| Teaching Facility?   Y/N |
| Traveler Friendly?   Y/N |
| Receive an Extension Offer? (YAY!!!!)     Y/N |
| Did you Accept the Extension Offer?   Y/N |
| Would you return? Y/N |

Travel Agency: _____     Recruiter: _____

Recruiter Contact Info: _____     _____
                                    (phone)                                            (e-mail)

Contract Duration _____ weeks

Additional Contract weeks extended _____

Charting System Used: _____ Charge Nurse Experience? Y / N

Floated to These Units: _____

Facility Address:

Enjoy Life!

*I was here....*

My temporary home address was....

**BEST** parts about this assignment:

➢

➢

➢

*Wherever you go becomes a part of you somehow.*

*-Anita Desai*

# Assignment No. _____

Facility Name: _____

Location: _____

Department: _____

Dates: _____

| Magnet Hospital?   Y/N |
| Teaching Facility?   Y/N |
| Traveler Friendly?   Y/N |
| Receive an Extension Offer? (YAY!!!!)     Y/N |
| Did you Accept the Extension Offer?   Y/N |
| Would you return? Y/N |

Travel Agency: _____    Recruiter: _____

Recruiter Contact Info: _____    _____

                (phone)                   (e-mail)

Contract Duration _____ weeks

Additional Contract weeks extended _____

Charting System Used: _____    Charge Nurse Experience? Y / N

Floated to These Units: _____

Facility Address:

*I was here....*

My temporary home address was....

**BEST** parts about this assignment:

➢

➢

➢

*Leave the world a better place.*

*– Sarah Thomas*

# Assignment No. _____

Magnet Hospital?   Y/N

Teaching Facility?   Y/N

Traveler Friendly?  Y/N

Receive an Extension
Offer? (YAY!!!!)     Y/N

Did you Accept the
Extension Offer?   Y/N

Would you return? Y/N

Facility Name:   _____

Location:   _____

Department: _____

Dates: _____

Travel Agency: _____   Recruiter: _____

Recruiter Contact Info: _____   _____
                                (phone)                                          (e-mail)

Contract Duration _____ weeks

Additional Contract weeks extended _____

Charting System Used: _____   Charge Nurse Experience? Y / N

Floated to These Units: _____

Facility Address:

I was here....

My temporary home address was....

BEST parts about this assignment:

➢

➢

➢

*I'll never understand the medical mind.*

*– Spock*

# Assignment No. _____

Facility Name: _____

Location: _____

Department: _____

Dates: _____

| |
|---|
| Magnet Hospital?   Y/N |
| Teaching Facility?   Y/N |
| Traveler Friendly?   Y/N |
| Receive an Extension Offer? (YAY!!!!)     Y/N |
| Did you Accept the Extension Offer?   Y/N |
| Would you return? Y/N |

Travel Agency: _____   Recruiter: _____

Recruiter Contact Info: _____   _____

(phone)                                      (e-mail)

Contract Duration _____ weeks

Additional Contract weeks extended _____

Charting System Used: _____   Charge Nurse Experience? Y / N

Floated to These Units: _____

Facility Address:

*I was here....*

My temporary home address was....

**BEST** parts about this assignment:

> 

> 

> 

*Focus on your potential instead of your limitations.*

*- Alan Loy McGinnis*

# Assignment No. _____

Facility Name: _____

Location: _____

Department: _____

Dates: _____

| | |
|---|---|
| Magnet Hospital?  Y/N | |
| Teaching Facility?  Y/N | |
| Traveler Friendly?  Y/N | |
| Receive an Extension Offer? (YAY!!!!)    Y/N | |
| Did you Accept the Extension Offer?   Y/N | |
| Would you return? Y/N | |

Travel Agency: _____   Recruiter: _____

Recruiter Contact Info: _____   _____

(phone)                                        (e-mail)

Contract Duration _____ weeks

Additional Contract weeks extended _____

Charting System Used: _____  Charge Nurse Experience? Y / N

Floated to These Units: _____

Facility Address:

# I was here....

My temporary home address was....

**BEST** parts about this assignment:

➢

➢

➢

*No act of kindness, no mater how small, is ever wasted.*

*– Aesop*

# Assignment No. ____

Facility Name: _____

Location: _____

Department: _____

Dates: _____

Magnet Hospital?   Y/N

Teaching Facility?   Y/N

Traveler Friendly?   Y/N

Receive an Extension Offer? (YAY!!!!)     Y/N

Did you Accept the Extension Offer?   Y/N

Would you return? Y/N

Travel Agency: _____  Recruiter: _____

Recruiter Contact Info: _____  _____
                        (phone)                        (e-mail)

Contract Duration _____ weeks

Additional Contract weeks extended _____

Charting System Used: _____  Charge Nurse Experience? Y / N

Floated to These Units: _____

Facility Address:

enjoy it all.

*I was here....*

My temporary home address was....

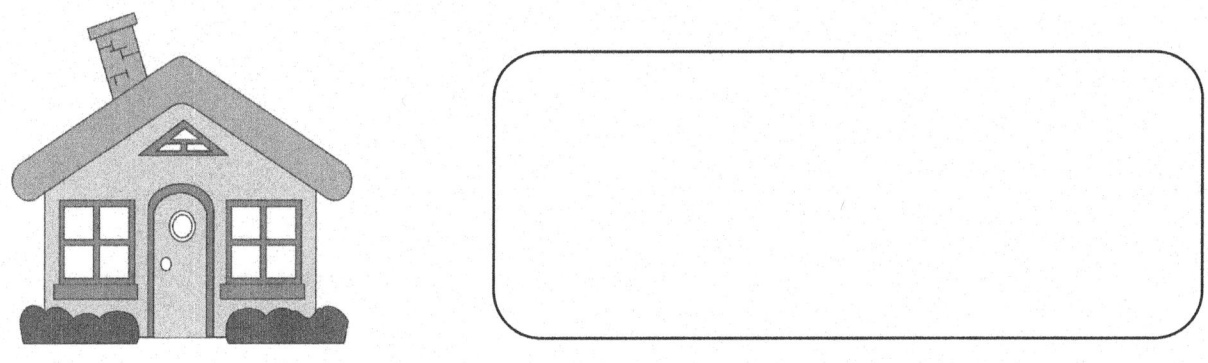

**BEST** parts about this assignment:

➢

➢

➢

*Giving is living. If you stop wanting to give, there's nothing more to live for. – Audrey Hepburn*

# Assignment No. _____

Facility Name: _____

Location: _____

Department: _____

Dates: _____

Magnet Hospital?   Y/N

Teaching Facility?   Y/N

Traveler Friendly?  Y/N

Receive an Extension
Offer? (YAY!!!!)     Y/N

Did you Accept the
Extension Offer?   Y/N

Would you return? Y/N

Travel Agency: _____     Recruiter: _____

Recruiter Contact Info: _____     _____

(phone)                                        (e-mail)

Contract Duration _____ weeks

Additional Contract weeks extended _____

Charting System Used: _____     Charge Nurse Experience? Y / N

Floated to These Units: _____

Facility Address:

*I was here....*

My temporary home address was....

**BEST** parts about this assignment:

➢

➢

➢

*Whatever you are, be a good one.*

*- Abraham Lincoln*

# Assignment No. _____

Magnet Hospital?   Y/N

Teaching Facility?   Y/N

Traveler Friendly?   Y/N

Receive an Extension Offer? (YAY!!!!)     Y/N

Did you Accept the Extension Offer?   Y/N

Would you return? Y/N

Facility Name: _____

Location: _____

Department: _____

Dates: _____

Travel Agency: _____   Recruiter: _____

Recruiter Contact Info: _____   _____

                                        (phone)                                                        (e-mail)

Contract Duration _____ weeks

Additional Contract weeks extended _____

Charting System Used: _____   Charge Nurse Experience? Y / N

Floated to These Units: _____

Facility Address:

I was here....

My temporary home address was....

**BEST** parts about this assignment:

➤

➤

➤

*Shoot for the moon. Even if you miss, you'll land among the stars. – Les Brown*

# Assignment No. _____

Magnet Hospital?   Y/N

Teaching Facility?   Y/N

Traveler Friendly?  Y/N

Receive an Extension
Offer? (YAY!!!!)     Y/N

Did you Accept the
Extension Offer?   Y/N

Would you return? Y/N

Facility Name: _____

Location: _____

Department: _____

Dates: _____

Travel Agency: _____  Recruiter: _____

Recruiter Contact Info: _____  _____
                              (phone)                                    (e-mail)

Contract Duration _____ weeks

Additional Contract weeks extended _____

Charting System Used: _____  Charge Nurse Experience? Y / N

Floated to These Units: _____

Facility Address:

*I was here....*

My temporary home address was....

**BEST** parts about this assignment:

➢

➢

➢

*Happiness can be found even in the darkest of times if only one remembers to turn on the light.  – Albus Dumbledore*

# Assignment No. _____

Facility Name: _____

Location: _____

Department: _____

Dates: _____

| Magnet Hospital?   Y/N |
| Teaching Facility?   Y/N |
| Traveler Friendly?  Y/N |
| Receive an Extension Offer? (YAY!!!!)     Y/N |
| Did you Accept the Extension Offer?   Y/N |
| Would you return? Y/N |

Travel Agency: _____   Recruiter: _____

Recruiter Contact Info: _____   _____
                              (phone)                              (e-mail)

Contract Duration _____ weeks

Additional Contract weeks extended _____

Charting System Used: _____   Charge Nurse Experience? Y / N

Floated to These Units: _____

Facility Address:

thank you

I was here....

My temporary home address was....

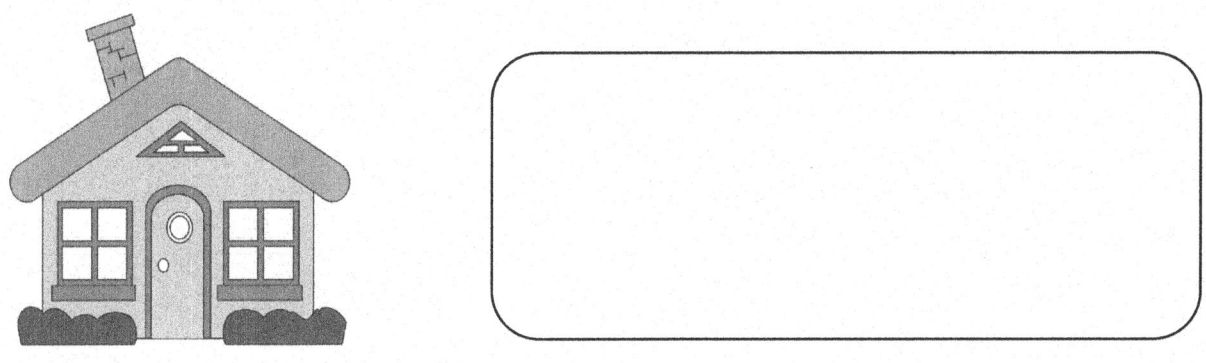

BEST parts about this assignment:

➢

➢

➢

I do one thing at a time. I do it very well...and then I move on. – Major Charles Emerson Winchester, MASH

# Assignment No. _____

Facility Name: _____

Location: _____

Department: _____

Dates: _____

Magnet Hospital?   Y/N

Teaching Facility?   Y/N

Traveler Friendly?  Y/N

Receive an Extension
Offer? (YAY!!!!)     Y/N

Did you Accept the
Extension Offer?   Y/N

Would you return? Y/N

Travel Agency: _____   Recruiter: _____

Recruiter Contact Info: _____   _____

(phone)                                    (e-mail)

Contract Duration _____ weeks

Additional Contract weeks extended _____

Charting System Used: _____  Charge Nurse Experience? Y / N

Floated to These Units: _____

Facility Address:

78

*I was here....*

My temporary home address was....

**BEST** parts about this assignment:

➢

➢

➢

*Integrity is doing the right thing. Even when no one is watching. – C.S. Lewis*

# Assignment No. _____

Magnet Hospital?   Y/N

Teaching Facility?   Y/N

Traveler Friendly?   Y/N

Receive an Extension
Offer? (YAY!!!!)     Y/N

Did you Accept the
Extension Offer?   Y/N

Would you return? Y/N

Facility Name:   _____

Location:   _____

Department: _____

Dates: _____

Travel Agency: _____  Recruiter: _____

Recruiter Contact Info: _____  _____
                                    (phone)                              (e-mail)

Contract Duration _____ weeks

Additional Contract weeks extended _____

Charting System Used: _____  Charge Nurse Experience? Y / N

Floated to These Units: _____

Facility Address:

you
make a
A DIFFERENCE

*I was here....*

My temporary home address was....

**BEST** parts about this assignment:

➢

➢

➢

*It's about the journey – mine and yours – and the lives we can touch,
the legacy we can leave, and the world we can change for the better.*

*–Tony Dungy*

# Assignment No. _____

Facility Name: _____

Location: _____

Department: _____

Dates: _____

Magnet Hospital?   Y/N

Teaching Facility?   Y/N

Traveler Friendly?  Y/N

Receive an Extension
Offer? (YAY!!!!)     Y/N

Did you Accept the
Extension Offer?   Y/N

Would you return? Y/N

Travel Agency: _____  Recruiter: _____

Recruiter Contact Info: _____  _____
                                (phone)                              (e-mail)

Contract Duration _____ weeks

Additional Contract weeks extended _____

Charting System Used: _____  Charge Nurse Experience? Y / N

Floated to These Units: _____

Facility Address:

you
are
awesome

*I was here....*

My temporary home address was....

**BEST** parts about this assignment:

> 

> 

> 

*Pray like it all depends on God, but work like it all depends on you. - Dave Ramsey*

# Assignment No. ____

Facility Name:  _____

Location:  _____

Department:  _____

Dates:  _____

Magnet Hospital?   Y/N

Teaching Facility?   Y/N

Traveler Friendly?  Y/N

Receive an Extension
Offer? (YAY!!!!)     Y/N

Did you Accept the
Extension Offer?   Y/N

Would you return? Y/N

Travel Agency: _____  Recruiter: _____

Recruiter Contact Info: _____  _____

              (phone)                      (e-mail)

Contract Duration _____ weeks

Additional Contract weeks extended _____

Charting System Used: _____  Charge Nurse Experience? Y / N

Floated to These Units: _____

Facility Address:

you ARE strong

*I was here....*

My temporary home address was....

**BEST** parts about this assignment:

➢

➢

➢

*He who would travel happily must travel light.*

*- Antoine de St. Exupery*

# Assignment No. _____

Facility Name: _____

Location: _____

Department: _____

Dates: _____

<table>
<tr><td>Magnet Hospital?   Y/N</td></tr>
<tr><td>Teaching Facility?   Y/N</td></tr>
<tr><td>Traveler Friendly?  Y/N</td></tr>
<tr><td>Receive an Extension Offer? (YAY!!!!)    Y/N</td></tr>
<tr><td>Did you Accept the Extension Offer?   Y/N</td></tr>
<tr><td>Would you return? Y/N</td></tr>
</table>

Travel Agency: _____   Recruiter: _____

Recruiter Contact Info: _____  _____
                              (phone)                                    (e-mail)

Contract Duration _____ weeks

Additional Contract weeks extended _____

Charting System Used: _____  Charge Nurse Experience? Y / N

Floated to These Units: _____

Facility Address:

take a Small Step EVERYDAY

*I was here....*

My temporary home address was....

**BEST** parts about this assignment:

➢

➢

➢

*The best way to find yourself is to lose yourself in the service of others. – Mahatma Ghandi*

# Assignment No. ____

Facility Name: _____

Location: _____

Department: _____

Dates: _____

Magnet Hospital?   Y/N

Teaching Facility?   Y/N

Traveler Friendly?   Y/N

Receive an Extension Offer? (YAY!!!!)     Y/N

Did you Accept the Extension Offer?   Y/N

Would you return? Y/N

Travel Agency: _____   Recruiter: _____

Recruiter Contact Info: _____   _____

             (phone)                      (e-mail)

Contract Duration _____ weeks

Additional Contract weeks extended _____

Charting System Used: _____   Charge Nurse Experience? Y / N

Floated to These Units: _____

Facility Address:

I was here....

My temporary home address was....

**BEST** parts about this assignment:

➤

➤

➤

*Never let the fear of striking out keep you from playing the game. – Babe Ruth*

# Assignment No. _____

Facility Name: _____

Location: _____

Department: _____

Dates: _____

Magnet Hospital?  Y/N

Teaching Facility?  Y/N

Traveler Friendly?  Y/N

Receive an Extension
Offer? (YAY!!!!)    Y/N

Did you Accept the
Extension Offer?   Y/N

Would you return? Y/N

Travel Agency: _____    Recruiter: _____

Recruiter Contact Info: _____    _____

                            (phone)                                 (e-mail)

Contract Duration _____ weeks

Additional Contract weeks extended _____

Charting System Used: _____    Charge Nurse Experience? Y / N

Floated to These Units: _____

Facility Address:

*I was here....*

My temporary home address was....

**BEST** parts about this assignment:

➢

➢

➢

*Being beautiful has very little to do with how you look.*

*- Stacie Martin*

# Assignment No. _____

Facility Name: _____

Location: _____

Department: _____

Dates: _____

| |
|---|
| Magnet Hospital?   Y/N |
| Teaching Facility?   Y/N |
| Traveler Friendly?   Y/N |
| Receive an Extension Offer? (YAY!!!!)     Y/N |
| Did you Accept the Extension Offer?   Y/N |
| Would you return? Y/N |

Travel Agency: _____   Recruiter: _____

Recruiter Contact Info: _____   _____
                                    (phone)                                    (e-mail)

Contract Duration _____ weeks

Additional Contract weeks extended _____

Charting System Used: _____ Charge Nurse Experience? Y / N

Floated to These Units: _____

Facility Address:

I was here....

My temporary home address was....

**BEST** parts about this assignment:

➤

➤

➤

Sometimes you will never know the value of a moment, until it becomes a memory.  – Dr. Seuss

# My Top Five Assignments

Of all the places you've been blessed to experience, which ones would you return to, hands down? (Remember to consider food, traffic and shopping options.)

Here are your top picks at a glance.

You may want to use pencil; favorites are subject to change!

1.

2.

3.

4.

5.

*Today me will live in the moment unless it's unpleasant in which case me will eat a cookie.*

*– Cookie Monster*

# References

If you chose to move to a permanent staff position or to work with a different agency, you will need references from facilities within the past six months to a year. List at least one from each location. Remember to **always** leave on good terms; you never know when you may need this reference!

Name:______________________________ Title:______________

Hospital & Location:______________________________________

Phone Number:____________________ E-mail:__________________

Name:______________________________ Title:______________

Hospital & Location:______________________________________

Phone Number:____________________ E-mail:__________________

Name:______________________________ Title:______________

Hospital & Location:______________________________________

Phone Number:____________________ E-mail:__________________

Name:______________________________ Title:______________

Hospital & Location:______________________________________

Phone Number:____________________ E-mail:__________________

�֍ Name:_____ Title:_____

Hospital & Location:_____

Phone Number:_____ E-mail:_____

�֍ Name:_____ Title:_____

Hospital & Location:_____

Phone Number:_____ E-mail:_____

✖ Name:_____ Title:_____

Hospital & Location:_____

Phone Number:_____ E-mail:_____

✖ Name:_____ Title:_____

Hospital & Location:_____

Phone Number:_____ E-mail:_____

✖ Name:_____ Title:_____

Hospital & Location:_____

Phone Number:_____ E-mail:_____

✖ Name:_____ Title:_____

Hospital & Location:_____

Phone Number:_____ E-mail:_____

# About the Author

Karie has been a nurse for over four years. At the conclusion of year no. 2, and after much prayer by her and her hubs, they decided to set out and go wherever God needed them. To this day they continue to travel to communities across the country with their dog, Higgins. Prayers for safe travels and for future patients and churches they will encounter are appreciated.

If you have any questions regarding the joys of traveling or how to become a Christian, please contact her at:

EternalEnterprizes@hotmail.com

Thank you for being a part of the journey!

Always pass on what you have learned.

– Yoda

There's so many strange places I'd like to be, But none of them permanently.

— Ernie, Sesame Street